SEVEN HANDS ◆ SEVEN HEARTS

SEVEN HANDS
SEVEN HEARTS

Elizabeth Woody

Drawings by Jaune Quick-to-See Smith

The Eighth Mountain Press

Portland ◆ Oregon ◆ 1994

Drawings by Jaune Quick-to-See Smith
Cover art by Rick Bartow: "Wajima Hawk" 1992
Cover design by Ruth Gundle
Book design by Ruth Gundle
Technical and design assistance: Roberta Lampert and Thad Laughlin

Manufactured in the United States of America
This book is printed on acid-free paper.
First edition 1994
10 9 8 7 6 5 4 3 2 1

LIBRARY OF CONGRESS CATALOGING-IN-PUBLICATION DATA
Woody, Elizabeth, 1959-
     Seven hands, seven hearts / Elizabeth Woody ; drawings by
  Jaune Quick-to-See Smith. — 1st ed.
          p.   cm.
     ISBN 0-933377-31-2 (alk. paper) : $22.95. — ISBN 0-933377-30-4 (pbk.)
     (alk. paper) : $13.95
     1. Indians of North America—Oregon—Literary collections. 2. Indians of
  North America—Women—Literary collections. 3. Women—Oregon—
  Literary collections. I. Title.
  PS3573.06455S48   1994
  818'.5409—dc20   94-32230

THE EIGHTH MOUNTAIN PRESS
624 Southeast Twenty-ninth Avenue
Portland, Oregon 97214
(503) 233-3936

ACKNOWLEDGMENTS

GRATEFUL ACKNOWLEDGMENT is made to the editors of the following magazines and anthologies in which these poems and stories first appeared or were reprinted. "She Is a Stranger to Intimacy" was first published in *Tyuonyi*; "Hand into Stone" was first published in *Faces of a Reservation* by Cynthia Stowell, Oregon Historical Society Press; "Siamese Ghosts (The Disturbed Spirits)" and "The Sense" were first published in *Spawning the Medicine River*; "Custer Must Have Learned to Dance" and "Black Fear" were first published in *Songs from This Earth on Turtle's Back*, edited by Joseph Bruchac, Greenfield Review Press; "Originating Fire" and "Of Steps to Drowning" were first published in *The Clouds Threw This Light*, edited by Phillip Foss, Institute of American Indian Arts Press; "Speaking Hands" was first published in *Calyx*; "Water Combined With Throat Singing" was first published in Wilderness Magazine. "Our Reverence and Difficult Return" was first published in *Akwekon*; "A Warrior and the Glass Prisoners" was first published in *Akwekon* and then reprinted in *Contact II*; "Spider Woman's Coyote Bones" was first published in *The Wooster Review*; "Hand into Stone," "In Memory of Crossing the Columbia," and "Of Steps to Drowning" were reprinted in *Dancing on the Rim of the World: An Anthology of Contemporary Northwest Native American Writing* edited by Andrea Lerner, University of Arizona Press; "In Memory of Crossing the Columbia," was also reprinted in *Home Places*, edited by Ofelia Zepeda and Larry Evers, University of Arizona Press;

"Reminiscent of Salmon Woman" and "The Bridge" were originally published in *Durable Breath: Contemporary Native American Poetry* edited by John Smelcer and D.L. Birchfield, Salmon Run Press/ American Indian Press; "Homecooking" was first published in *Talking Leaves: Contemporary Native American Short Stories,* edited by Craig Lesley, Dell/Laurel; "Buckskin" was originally published in *Oregon Heritage.*

The poems in the third section, "Hand into Stone" were originally published as a collection, *Hand into Stone,* by Contact II Publications in 1988 and won the American Book Award from the Before Columbus Foundation in 1990.

I wish to express my gratitude to Ruth Gundle for providing me with the opportunity to reprint *Hand into Stone.* The new work in *Seven Hands, Seven Hearts* was written with her encouragement and discerning editorship. I wish to thank Lillian Pitt, who has provided me with the essentials I needed to continue with the writing of poetry and my art, especially the courage.

TABLE OF CONTENTS

III. Hand into Stone

TO MY PARENTS:
Charlotte Pitt and Guy Woody

and

TO MY TEACHERS:
those I've encountered in formal education
and those who have taught me as I've made my way in life

INTRODUCTION

MY CHILDHOOD HOME was fourteen miles from the Warm Springs Reservation, in the town of Madras, Oregon. We were over a hundred miles from the Columbia River and the pathways of the salmon that my mother's people cherished, celebrated, harvested, dried, and incorporated into their lifeways for over fourteen thousand years. Although we were removed from our ancestral homeland of the Columbia River system, that landscape—the snowcapped Cascade range of volcanoes, surrounded by evergreen forests and high desert—is still an integral element of the culture of the Plateau Columbia River people, as we are collectively called. I belong to a people who cherish the land.

My maternal grandparents were the first of several generations to be born within the reservation boundaries formed by the Treaty of 1855 between "the Bostons" (so called because after dealing with the English and French, the Plateau people considered the United States an infant and unreliable government) and the people presently known, in part, as the Warm Springs, Yakama, Umatilla, Spokane, and Nez Perce tribes. We had not called our people "tribes" prior to the treaty; it is a term brought from feudal Europe. Plateau societies were characterized as such because participants who shared political principles lived in a village governed by a leader who was not subject to outside authority. Decisions were made by acclamation, and those who disagreed moved to another village.

My grandfather, Lewis Pitt, Sr., was of Wasco/Wishram/

Watlala/Welsh descent. These fishing people made distinctive art objects depicting "X-ray figures"—female and male—of people, ancient sturgeon, condor, and deer. My grandmother, Elizabeth Thompson Pitt, a descendant of the Wyampum and a smaller Deschutes River band, Tygh, was born and raised at the hot springs now known as Kah-nee-ta Resort. She was as settled on this land as the old junipers, the volcanic formations, and hillsides that she loved to walk about on. She was an artisan and possibly, for a time, a healer. She made sure that I understood her reverence for the land and the traditional beliefs by taking me as a child to the places where the people gathered for worship—places still filled with symbolism and ceremony.

My grandfather was an "Agency" man, my grandmother a "Simnasho" woman. Agency and Simnasho were two distinct cultural communities on the reservation: two small gatherings of longhouses and houses, churches and tule shacks, the families and their animals. When my grandparents married, each planted a cedar tree, side by side. The trees intermingled their roots and boughs, symbolizing the tentative touchings of two separate beings. In the longhouses and homes of both settlements one could hear all the different languages spoken by the group and their visitors. My grandfather spoke six dialects of Sahaptin and Chinookan Northwest indigenous languages as well as the intertribal trade language, Chinook Jargon. My grandmother spoke Warm Springs/Sahaptin in her own distinctive way. They brought to their speech a passion for expression, and in that passion, a love for all things.

In Warm Springs, in a place referred to as "Hollywood," my grandparents' home was always open and often filled with people eating, telling stories, laughing, making music, or having discussions. My Aunt Lillian recalls that there seemed to be no sense of time as we think of it. People would be sleeping on blankets on the floor while others were seeking advice from one another. When the sleepers got up, others would lie down. Everyone worked, ate, and slept when it felt right—on their own schedules—while maintaining an essential connection to the group. When I think of that house, I feel near the fire of intensity that warmed their efforts to survive the maelstrom of our dispossession.

In the 1950s my grandparents moved off the reservation to be nearer to their three children's high school, where only English was spoken. While my grandfather commuted daily to work in Warm Springs, my grandmother was distanced from the beading circles, healing gatherings, celebrations, winter dances, and the casual visiting at the general store/post office. My Uncle Lewis, Jr., recalls that she took refuge in her bedroom. Her room held the many bundles of beaded objects, cornhusk bags, and Klickitat baskets we inherited from our ancestors. It seemed that to visit these things was to contact the thoughts of those who had passed on. Finally, one day, the house brightened when she decided to make some leggings. For the first time alone, she drew her pattern and started beading. She asked Lewis, Jr., "Do you like my leggings?" He was ecstatic. "Yes," he said, "they are beautiful." He knew at that moment, by the startling burst of her creativity, in her pleasant circle of light, that they would be all right in their new home.

It is this blessing of being able to make things to remember and give away that gives me the knowledge of how to restore myself. The handwork of antiquity—the buckskin garments, the beaded objects, the woven baskets for subsistence, the cradleboards for protection, the feathers, the couriers to a higher thought—were made, traded, and collected by my great-grandparents and by my living relatives. The messages encoded in the designs (beaded birds, horses, trees, stars, and geometric abstractions) are like prayers, prayers for our present world to know again the root connection to our existence. All these objects were made from the earth and did not disrupt its systems. They embodied the belief that the earth provides for us, and through the earth we prosper and absorb into ourselves the potency of life.

And it is through my own story and the stories of my family and my circle of people that I become whole. I learned this as a child. At gatherings—whether in traditional settings such as the longhouse or simply in our kitchen—stories would roll out and encircle the group. From each telling we would become strengthened, released from a sense of isolation. We fed ourselves with these stories that explored how to live and that told of the past. The skill of telling and listening was "handed down," a legacy from a very ancient art form of imparting and storing knowledge and wisdom. It requires patience to listen to hours of "testimony." And one must learn to listen without judgment, overruling, interjection, or suppression.

These stories shape how I think, especially how I think of the land. My grandmother insisted that rocks had names and spirit. She passed on to me her belief that the land is imbued with spirit and unseen hosts. She heard the language of the earth. My grandparents loved to take drives just to look at the land. They would talk about the things they saw, which I could never really see.

In these stories I learned the meaning of being a granddaughter, a daughter, a niece, a sister, a cousin. I learned how to respect others and how to act with courage, humility, generosity, and compassion. Although this is simple to say in English and is overused in daily language, it is complex to be an independent being, responsible to the nuances and dynamics of ancestral continuity.

◆ ◆ ◆

It was United States government policy, until just a few years ago, to eradicate all Indian languages. It was illegal to teach them in schools. I am part of the generation in which this language massacre reached its final stage: I learned only English. But those older languages are active in my brain. Waking to the aroma of coffee, I listened as a child to the Indian words of my grandmother and great-aunt in the morning. I also heard the softness of their walk and the song accompanying them from the birds in the junipers. Such simple pleasures elude me to this day, but the memory returns stronger as I grow older. Even though I've had to become proficient in a language and speaking style entirely different from that of my Sahaptin-Wasco-Diné ancestors, I believe the language I use in my poetry comes from the deep well of these ancient American languages. Listening to the older aspects of myself in my relatives, I was initiated into a life's work with words.

I am also part of the generation in which the possibility of regaining those languages has occurred. I could, for example, learn Salish, Sahaptin, or Diné at a university from fluent speakers. Interactive computer programs are being developed specifically for Native languages. One can hear, see, read, and learn to write them (even though they were not originally written languages). This is meaningful not only to me and to other Native Americans like me who have been deprived of their languages. A culture can't survive without its language; the loss of any language makes a gaping hole in world culture.

After speaking about artistic collaboration at a recent conference, a Wasco "aunty" told me, "Collaboration, in our language, is also the word for science." I feel that this includes nature, which holds everything and which directs the patterned chaos and the tranquillity of being complete, even in its smallest form. I have heard from people who are Native speakers that to use their language is to be more efficient in thinking. One Inupiaq man who has several advanced degrees said to a friend, "It's a shame you don't know your own language. It would allow you to comprehend the universe with a much greater conceptual capacity." Eradication of Native languages through colonization has impacted massive stores of knowledge.

◆ ◆ ◆

I have been learning to weave root bags. It requires a thought process I've been in need of for a long time. It claimed me, coming from women on both sides of my family who are weavers: my Navajo grandmother Annie Woody wove rugs; my Warm Springs grandmother Elizabeth Pitt wove cornhusk bags and root bags. My teacher, Margaret Jim-Pennah, told me during my apprenticeship as we sat twining, "We are making beautiful houses for our little sisters." I paused, then asked, "Who are our little sisters?" "The roots—the *pia-xi, khoush, sowit-k, wak amu,*" she answered. As we wove, I felt like a child again. While attempting to bead, I had shown my first clumsy rosettes to my grandmother. She looked at them and said that I was an expert already. I threw the rosettes in the trash but she dug them out, sewed safety pins to the back, and wore them on her sweater.

I worry that I cannot master these traditions, that I am too old to train myself away from what I was forced to learn to fit into the larger world. Margaret says, "Don't worry—weave!" It seems that I grow stronger by practicing this craft. I've learned from Margaret that to make things with the earth is a way of nourishing ourselves. We acknowledge our roots in the earth. We must remember our source of nourishment or we will starve.

Through my awareness of my history, tradition is alive. I can see my place as a responsible link in a dynamic process. My work embodies tradition, not as static dogma, but as public devotion to the continuation and enrichment of "the People." I look to the vitality of imagination manifest as the Earth, Homeland, and House of Livelihood and Rest. All around the story, eyes look into the sway of industrious endeavor, our hands move back to the beginning each time we work with material from the land. We listen, absorbed in the story by blood, by association, listening with the part that is both one self and many selves. In the sound of water, the sheen of river rock—a song, a poem, a story—is faithful to continuance.

I

BY OUR HAND, THROUGH MEMORY, THE HOUSE IS MORE THAN FORM

BUCKSKIN

BUCKSKIN WAS A YELLOWISH-TAN behemoth, a '76 Galaxy 500 automobile. The family loved her. We still talk about the beast with affection. At best, she carried us all up the deeply rutted, dirt road on the mountainside to Lester's remote cabin with ease. No dragging on bottom, the springs agile and strong. At worst, her transmission linkages popped out of place, once during a manic Seattle rush-hour crisis. When this happened, Leslie would have to coast to a stop, jump out, hoist the hood, reach into the engine, balance on her solar plexus, skirt and legs up in the air, and pop the mechanism into its socket, check the hanger wires, then run like crazy back into the driver's seat. The name Buckskin was chosen, not to honor our Native American heritage, but because she was a bona fide, temperamental, restless warhorse, an Indian car. In that legacy, she had to earn her name.

Buckskin was faithful, with a face that only a mother could love, big enough to haul four thirty-gallon garbage cans, and on occasion two or three generations of Palmers. The Palmers are big, no matter the age or gender (I am a good example of our size: six foot four inches, long black hair and round, a mountain of womanhood I have heard from my admirers—big, brown, and beautiful). But back to my love story.

This is a story of love between a family and a car. Brief, true, and bittersweet, like all those sad occurrences when people meet their match and circumstances wrench them apart.

Buckskin was a "spirit" car. When one of us was blue—like Leslie, or SugarMom, or Tone, or Gladys (better known as Happy Butt)— we would plan a trip to a powwow or celebration, load up all the camping gear, dance outfits, cans of oil, in the massive space of the trunk, gas up, and go. Nothing but a song and prayer, and the ingenuity of our collective genius, the product of the "make do" school. You see, when we first acquired Buckskin, we had been carless for years. Tone said, "Yeah, she's going to be a collector's item one of these days. She's a tank. A good old-fashioned American gas-hog. God love her! Now we can go anywhere!" Of course, he was the first to groan when her parts started to wear out and drop off. Like any mechanic's bread and butter, her parts wore out or dropped off at inappropriate times. Tone and I were driving down "Sideburn"—the nickname we had for Burnside—during another typical Northwest squall, and Buckskin flipped off her wiper, driver's side. I clutched the seat, and Tone hollered as he looked at me, "Now what?"

"Pull over, Tone. We can't drive without a wiper, 'less you want to stick your head out," which was our previous solution in cars back. Tone ran and picked up the wiper. We weren't savvy enough to all of Buckskin's ways then, so we didn't have any hangers in the car. I had a buckskin tie holding my hair, so I offered it to Tone. He rigged up a tie for the wiper. When we related the incident to SugarMom, who was angry, waiting downtown in the rain for us, she exclaimed in merriment, "Buckskin! Yeah, that's a good name for her. What a gal!" SugarMom's mood changed for the better by the event of Buckskin's naming.

So Buckskin became a character, well known, and all on her own. We learned how far we could go on the gas gauge's "E." We lovingly cleaned her carburetor so she wouldn't stall. The kids squealed with delight as she backfired, resounding in the streets like a shotgun, "Look at all the birds take off!" We offered everyone a ride who needed one, a ride they would never forget. She could go with ease down the freeway to Celilo Village at eighty, no problem, nondescript, maybe even invisible to the "smokies" (state patrol). She even had a sister car at Ace Wrecking Yards to donate parts to her in emergencies. One of our many Indian mechanics said, "The way her vinyl top is ripped off, it looks like Buckskin has a giant skid mark on top. Ha, ha, ha!" Since he was laughing at her and not with her, we dropped him off our list of mechanics. Eventually, he just left town.

Buckskin became a celebrity. Sadly, the most important trip was the trip that did her in. She came through for us, even though her front end was going out. We needed to go to Lewiston, Idaho, to rescue Leslie from out-of-state justice. We drove carefully, made it in time to hear the police chief testify to Leslie's actions that led to her arrest. It was hard not to burst into outrage as he exaggerated a description of Leslie screaming a karate yell, leaping ten feet to kick the officer in the groin, and finally slash him with her house keys. Of course, Leslie was acquitted since they had no evidence of a lethal weapon, and we rode home, triumphant, in Buckskin, laughingly teasing Leslie, calling her "Leslie Lee" after Bruce Lee.

Buckskin was with us "all the way," as they say on the rez—a true-blood. So it hurt when we realized that we couldn't keep her any longer. Too much of our energies were tied up in willing her to keep running, so we could keep on with our rescue missions when one of our clan needed help. We had to trade her off at Chevy Town. SugarMom cried. Months later, Leslie reported a resurrected Buckskin to us, her whereabouts, in which direction she was heading. Always, we could tell it was her by the Indian head decal on her backside. It was like a tattoo of a past lover's name. It did take years to forget her faithfulness, in spite of her temper, backfires, and flat tires.

We have a Toyota now, White Buckskin '89. You have to count the clicks in the automatic transmission to get in gear, tell the passengers as fast as you can: *Don't roll the window down any farther than half, because the door pops open and you could roll out.* The "ejector seat," we call it. If you don't like your date, you can just ask him to roll down his window and then turn sharply to the left. When SugarMom brought her home, Tone said, "God, love 'em! Now we can go anywhere on a tank of gas!" Happy Butt said, "Oh jeeze, SugarMom, you bought a 'pop-together car,'" as she kicked the small tires and fingered the bumper. White Buckskin is an Indian car, though. A few more years and she will be broken in, just the way we like it.

HOMECOOKING

THE FLAT TEETH of the morning sun chew at the blisters of the old tar-papered house. In the garden that thrives under a cloak of sagging cheesecloth, the grasshoppers pose on the promise of a meal. Granma is framed in the kitchen window as the tongues of curtains remain out from the morning breeze. Even with the hollyhocks' colorful bonnets, up tight against the wall, the house can appear as barren as a piano without ivory. There is a swarm of colors about the screen door, of calicos, tabbies, sylvesters, and blackies. They mew for their meal, in a chorus. As I turn back the covers from my floor bed, I hear humming and a spoon scratching the sides of a pan.

Watching the swill of leftovers sop up the milk, Granma turns to take the pan to the cats, twenty-some wild ones. She is pleased to see me up so early and smiles a toothless greeting. "Hi, honey, got to feed my livestock." She sings her good-morning almost, in the sweet, high-voiced, rhythmic dialect of Warm Springs English that sounds Indian. She is no bigger than five feet and no more than ninety-eight pounds. I see her hook the cats in her path expertly with her toes to flip them aside, with a dancer's grace. I once had balked at Granpa's joke about putting up little goal posts in the yard, for Granma to improve her "cat-punting." That was some years ago. Now, I am oblivious to her harmless way of walking through the fur mass of cats that stay for the one meal and all the mice and grasshoppers they can eat in the garden.

As I settle at the table, I think of the music my grandmother makes, which evokes some aspect of the world I had forgotten since my last visit. Like toads slurping up great moths at night, or the ripple and tumble of water over the rocks in the river, that is how her songs sound to me. I breathe in the sweet smell of old age that lingers after my mother's mother. The Nivea, the cleanliness of air-dried cotton, the oiled hair. I notice two plump rainbow trout on the counter and move to clean them.

She returns quietly, upon seeing me work, tells me, "You can fry up those fish. Someone brought them over real early. One relative I don't know at all. All these kids look like strangers to me. I guess it's just old age that makes me forget how many of all you kids there are." She laughs a little as she looks to my response out of her eye-corners, sitting behind her coffee at the table.

"Oh, Granma," I say, and catching her mood, tease back, "I know you have to remember me. If not for my family resemblance, then just for the trouble you had to take to wind me so you could catch me and make me come inside from playing." I eye her, likewise with cornered eyes. I see her catch her coffee in her lips, in an effort to keep from spitting the liquid and by laughing encourage me. She responds quickly saying, "Your mother could outrun me." Usually, she ends this comment about my mother's great speed in childhood by saying that she was "just too tired to whip her for her naughtiness." Listening to the house groan in the ceiling, Granma changes the subject to the building of our ranch house up Tenino Valley.

"Your grandfather's people made that old ranch house over there. All from one tree. All the people came to do what they could. Pound the nails. Split the wood. The women butchered and barbecued the steers. Everyone helped then. They drug the tree there by horse team. Those days our people knew how to do everything for themselves. Not like nowadays, where we have to hire big shots to come in and boss us around."

The pan snaps from the wet skin of the fish as I begin to fry them up. I know that she did not witness the building of this ranch house. She has only merged her stories with my grandfather's, a merging they wanted, symbolized by the two cedar trees that they both planted, side by side, when they married. Saying to each other that these trees would grow together, like they would, intermingling their roots and branches as one, while still letting the winds of life blow between them. I say, to bring her back to the moment, "These are pretty trout, Granma. About as good as the ones we used to catch, that would make Granpa so mad, when I was a kid."

Granma reaches up to arrange the fold of her navy blue western bandanna on her head. It is folded, tricornered and knotted on top. She tilts her chin upward. "Oh, how he would get mad. He always said I had more luck than sense. I had a good dream about him last night. That he and I and Baby were fishing. Baby and I caught a fish, and then we were jumping up and down around it, squealing. Granpa said we were scaring away his fish. He always wanted the fish to just jump on his hook."

I laugh, "Granma, I must have been that baby. Sometimes I wish that we had some poles, so we could fish. But then, we never did learn how to tie a good knot for the hooks. Oh, how we chased the grasshoppers for bait. You laughed so hard at me, jumping as hard as the bugs. We just had to sit down in the cheat grass and hold our sides and our dresses close to our legs, so the grasshoppers wouldn't jump up on them. But what really got Granpa was the fish we caught, and you would just flip them up in the air behind us. He said that was no way to treat a fish."

Granma, nodding her head, continues the reminiscence. "We only used a pin hook and bait. He had to spend our money on the fancy lures, the steelhead poles. He had his science and some notion that he treated the fish better when he made some big game out of it. We just needed fish for our table, not for bragging. Your Granpa was a good man, even though he had a soft heart about killing things, like the deer."

The heat intensifies outside and the "hotbugs" sing their legs into a zzzzing without pause. Granma sips her coffee, intermittently stirs the spoon in her cup. She eyes the spiral and begins to dream, like she dreams during the day, between words.

These stories of old days are magical. I'm gullible and young enough to still believe in magic. The magic is this soft rumble of blood-life, laughter, our great heart under the land. I hear that great tree and the cedars breathe through this house, too, on occasion. Up the valley, I can see the mountain hold a cap of a cloud. That mountain is as storied as our lives. He walked, lived, and lusted after a young woman mountain, fought with Wy-East for her in a time way before the Changer came to have all this chaos beaded up into some monstrously big Dreamer design. The design I only sense from the perspective of a bead. Sometimes I dream of this. I see segments of this power hanging from the hands of old ladies as they dance at gatherings. When I told my boyfriend this, he just said I was too way-out for him. That's how he seems to be anymore. Despite all his singing, sweating, he's too heavy with war and struggle to see the story. Yet, love always seems to knock men down to drag them back to these houses of magic. Just like love knocks us down and pulls us out to the sticks, to follow that guy. Keep an eye on him, just in case something might take him away by terrible magic. Yes, the age of the Changer has passed, but the bloodline is still with us, and the inspiring thread of women's labor, the beads, the Great Transformer, and the talk of love. The Beautiful Woman in Earth still whispers into the ears of her children.

"Owww-witch!" I holler, as the grease sizzles on the skin of my hand. The fish get one last bite on me.

"Watch your cooking. You might just get as bad as me. I never got the hang of cooking on electric stoves. I always cooked on wood stoves or campfires. The first days I was married to your grandfather, we lived in a tent to put his brother through college, you know."

"Yeah, Gram. But I think it isn't your cooking abilities I inherited but the old Dreamer brain. I wasn't thinking about the fish in the pan."

At this point she chuckles deeply, nodding her head, which turns her bandanna a nudge-worth out of place. A meadowlark tinkles a song from the yard. She tilts her head, so her bandanna looks correct, and says, "He sings about the rain that will come soon. Of course, in Indian he makes his song. That's why it is so beautiful to me." She taps her finger on the handle of her eternal coffee cup. She waits, as she always waits, in a meditation. She waits through her chores. She waits for her children to come and visit as I visit, answering her call for company.

As I pull out the enamel, shallow-bowled dishes, I remain quiet so as not to interrupt the thoughts I see about her, probably a prayer. She responds to me out of courtesy, since her thoughts linger over her long life and the memories that are so necessary.

I again think about the music I hear. I hear songs in my dreams. Which is unusual, since I do not know any songs, or even know Indian. I think of it as this, the music comes from the tapping of her finger, beating out the occasional soft song. The way a river sounds while we fish, and the sound of the life—dragonflies whirring by, singing to me—the music mingles and makes these songs that sound through my dreams. Maybe I catch the hum of the mountain over there too. He's waiting, you see, to get involved with that fiery young woman he sees at the corner of his eyes. Mountain love is a real shaky, fired-up affair. They push up great hilly ranges, bed over the lakes, rub up against each other so wildly that it takes years to cover up all that passionate rumbling and love talk. Once my grandmother said that her great-great-grandmother and aunt had to run their horses into a lake and cover themselves with wet hides to keep from getting burned. The water was so hot, it took all their courage to stay put. I believe that was the last rumble before the mountains curled up for a good sleep.

When I told one of my science teachers about this, he said that these stories are just myth, not fact, and that mountains don't love or even erupt anymore. I believed him until Mount St. Helens erupted. It erased all innocent belief in the fable of absolutes in science for me. Thank goodness I had heard some fact about those mountains way before I entered school.

I give my grandmother her share of the fish, and she says as she always says, "Oh, honey, that is too much. Put some back. I'm not company."

"Eat, Granma, we have plenty for many lifetimes over." I settle my body down to savor the fish. "You know, I sure miss Granpa. I miss his whistling in the mornings. When you and him would cook together. You remember that?"

Granma retorts, "I have spent half of my life cooking for all of you. But it was your grandfather who could cook the best. He knew all the dishes of this and that. Just like he knew all that wild music. High-why-ahn, I think it was called. He was a great jokester. You tell a story as tall as he could, but I always thought you hung around him too much."

I smile, then say, "You both were pretty wild examples for me to follow. I think a lot about how you two would play in the kitchen, while you cooked what you called a farmer's breakfast, the potatoes, ham steaks, eggs. Between flipping over the food, you would dance to Western music on the transistor radio, the jitterbug, the Charleston. Yeah, I remember how you two carried on while you thought I was still asleep." I smile thinking of how agile Granma was, dancing, diaper pins on her dress, blue tennis shoes toeing in and out. Granpa, twirling her around, in his sleeveless white undershirt, pants always neatly belted, with a smile wide in pleasure, watching Granma's face spin like a light in the early dawn. Granpa had a grin so wide it was as if it could go halfway around his head, especially when he had Granma going or had her aggravated from teasing her. Then he'd grin all the more while he sweet-talked his way back into her good humor.

"It seemed that you always ended up your dancing with a good fight, boxing, with your dukes curled over. You always won with your Appalachian apple cut, half a wind up, a quick strike to Granpa's glass jaw. Then you'd grab his pants seat and have him at your mercy. He'd holler, 'I give up, honey! I give up, I'll marry you!'"

We both laughed a great laugh at the memory. Granma tucked the trout meat into a pouch in her soft cheek, tilted her chin toward me, and said in a quiet, matter-of-fact tone, "Your grandfather didn't marry me for my homecooking. I thought you always knew that."

STORY POWER

DAD WAS A CHRISTIAN man. He never said much about hardcore Christian things—not like my friends at the gospel church—except that his Bible was his way of talking with the divine. It seemed that he never much cared for us kids packing up to go with Mom to the traditional doings or healings. He knew we always fell asleep on the floor under the benches before anything started up or really got going. It's just that this outdoors man believed mystery was everywhere.

He was the kind of man who loved to sleep out, and then big old bull snakes or bullfrogs would climb up on his chest for the night. Probably to see where all the earth-shaking vibration was coming from. Daddy snored loud. He would even wake himself up yelling, "What's that?" and gently push away whatever creature had decided to curl up on him. He would tell us about it, later. He'd say, "It was so surprised to see itself sleeping on a man." That's his way of story.

"If you do need to tell a story," Dad would say, "it's best to leave some holes in it, somewhere." It's easier that way, since most of us know the story by having heard it before, or by having been there when it happened.

There were times when I was a kid, I'd be pulling my wagon to the woodpile. Dad would be standing there with Mom's Christmas axe, looking at the horizon. He would ask, "Henry, did you see anything unusual?" I would look at him, his dark plaid Pendleton shirt over his thermals, his work boots stitched up and tied in beautiful bows, his wavy black hair poking up from the rim of his stocking cap. I would look at his pressed gray twill pants, the Bulova watch on his left hand, and the wood axe handle in the right, the split wood on each side of the chopping block. None of this was strange at all. I would shake my head and say, "No, Daddy."

His face would tense. Then he would say something that would make my hair and scalp wiggle (he never spared me the details). "You didn't see that man on horseback ride through here?" I would say no, very gently, and pick up the wood to load into my red wagon. I pulled it back to the porch, looking everywhere, just in case I could catch a glimpse.

He was a man who by blood had this real strong visionary streak that never stopped reminding him of who he really was. He was not crazy or mean. In fact, his gentleness and smarts brought to him many devoted friends. He said there were angels and there were miracles occurring every day (but not at the rate the Catholics claim). Mom was a bit more dramatic and strong-voiced about visions. She would have had no problem sitting in a Buddhist monastery, davening in a synagogue, or ringing bells in a Shaker church, just so long as they were speaking about God. She was a great feeler. She always knew when deer would be coming. She didn't like handling a rifle, so if we needed venison, Daddy was the one who went to where it was supposed to be and brought it home to serve at the big dinner for a naming or celebration.

I was used to her way of knowing my thoughts and answering them, whether I asked or not. I always counted on her being direct and on the mark, more or less. She could say anything important in five words or less. Dad was the mystery. Sometimes he just made a story. I can't complete one of them whole, because I've forgotten some part for the sake of sparing myself from the vision coming to me. I have his blood moving through my heart, changing from red to blue. Man to woman, light and dark, this is the blood of nature. This is the story his mother taught him.

In the summer Dad and Mom would send me out to summer camp up at Bald Peter. They would leave me there with all the other reservation kids to learn the "way of the woods." We called it the "sticks," a term leftover from the old trade language of the river, Chinook Jargon. I thought it was a strange language, with its pidgin French and English mixed with other Indian languages. Dad talked it, along with the other complete languages that sounded pretty much like the land. The sounds made me think of mountains and wind, the echo of water, sharp angles and stops of the high desert light, and whisper of trees. It was in the sounds of language that I first heard about the "unknowable." Later, I learned about the "unknowable people," like the Stick Indians and the Bigfoot.

In our camp teepees at night the others would rev up and tell stories. The scary ghost stories were the leadup to the eventual face-to-face personal accounts of Stick Indians. How they were almost stolen by a Stick Indian when they were bad to their parents. It seemed that all the kids had run into them at the creek. I would listen and wiggle deep into my sleeping bag, clutching small pieces of fir needles from the outdoor mattress under me, the sweet smelling fir boughs.

By morning I would forget it all in the excitement of camp. Things were always happening, like the time a porcupine walked into the girls' outhouse. The youngest and prettiest counselor ran out, screaming, holding up her unzipped jeans. We chased that porcupine right out of camp. There were salamanders to watch out for and catch at the swimming hole, and the chipmunks were always ready to be chased. I made up stories about all these events. Mom and Dad liked my description of the small sweathouse, and of the squirrels playing, and how we would sometimes cook over an open campfire. I learned that the potpourri smell of strawberries in the woods meant little treats, if you looked for them and picked them. The creek was too cold this high up to have trout, but we saw one once. It was the only one. We wouldn't have fished for it even if we'd had our poles.

Dad once told me, "If you act like a fool out in the sticks, harm could come to you pretty quick. But to play is a natural thing, like those squirrels; everyone learns from happiness in some way." Dad said that I may not have played hard enough yet.

One day after I came back from camp I said to Dad, "Stories always hit me strong...." I paused, the silence unusual in the usual noise of supper, utensils on plates, the talk. Dad said, "Don't think bad of the unknowable, especially its people. Those disturbing stories you heard are not the whole story. Those 'wild looking' people saved my life once. If you are good, they can help you. You're innocent and watched over, anyway. Don't be afraid. Of the woods, especially, because that's our home too. We may live in town now, but we used to be there—wherever we needed to be to get our food and our medicine. I'll admit Indian medicine is powerful. Your aunty saved me with her medicine she made."

I nodded, remembering the story. Dad looked at my mother for approval. Her nod made him continue, "I used to make fun of those little people stories. Too much, I guess.

"I worked out at CCC Camp before I settled into being part of a family with your mother and her people. We'd tell scary stories to the white guys who never heard of the stick people before. Just to spook them. I never believed them, though.

"I was foreman and took the guys out for a hike. We made fire trails, sometimes we even had time to hunt for game. One day, on such a hike, I showed off and hung up a wild turkey in a tree, saying real loud, "For the little people." I looked at the men, checked their faces to see what effect I'd had on them. It's bad to brag, worse to lie. As we walked, I felt kinda strange. So, I sent them on ahead. I stayed back, feeling worse. I was lost and it started to snow! Then I did what is the worst thing to do in such a situation, I lay down to sleep, feeling warm. Snow and cold can do that to you.

"Well, I woke up in the dark on fir boughs under a lean-to, next to a fire. The fire had meat staked over it. It smelled good. I looked around, felt eyes looking at me, and jumped up real quick. I ran and ran. Right down the hill, right to camp. I had no trouble with my sense of direction then.

"I never told anyone about it except your mother. The guys ribbed me about hiking around all night like some kind of Bigfoot. Bigfoot's another story, though."

Mom chuckled. She bent over to me and said, "These very small and very large people are powerful in their way. They whistle too, Sonny. They help good hunters and you never know. Just be good to everyone and all things. You'll make it all right. You'll learn to love those mountains, if you don't have fear rattling in your mind, confusing you. You haven't yet heard the whole story."

II

SEVEN HANDS, SEVEN HEARTS

REMINISCENT OF SALMON WOMAN

Abalone swinging on the ears of Salmon Woman signals
the time to witness. The dance of budding camas flowers,
yellowtail butterflies and wild roses.
Spring in green and blue. Light moves water.
In one motion, dawn and dusk separate into daylight.
Salmon Mother at the head of stream, speaks.
The spawning rush of salmon tails makes space for roe and milt.
The salmon's precise eyes glisten.
Diamonds reflect dark carbon of age in the center.
The passage absorbs the deep voice of her renewal song.
The woman's mouth breaks through the surface of tranquillity.

WATER COMBINED WITH THROAT SINGING

Straining to hear the whisper of stones, bones tremble.
Ash blows into ears. White stars are closeted.
Rush of peace. Rush of snow. Mountains
tell of how songs melt into every being, above and below.

Hushed trees sleep from the past days' sun. Water
feels pleasant welling in the belly. Belly of heart.
Belly of nourishment. Well of drum. Mumble of dream.

Cedar trees hold out flat palms of several lives' lines,
several summers of rain in memory.
Summers of drought ring thin.
Cold is lack of birds flying and singing.

The character of brush is a different walk.
A cobalt blue pane is the mirror
of water absorbing sound. Wet night of flashes.
Thunder traces its echo in the flush of vision.

THE BRIDGE

The moon as woman rolls along handrails
that support a fine-boned fist of the woman in grief.
The moon, orange and alive with veins, rises slowly.
It pushes through skin.
As it rises a breath exhales.
As it rises someone moves inside.
The skin of the opening fist of her worn palm
shows the talcum dust of loss. Tears are dark spots.
She turns out her palm. It shimmers with light.
A circled halo, the substance of her love.
Love that she rubs onto that bridge like polish.

HORSE AND WOMAN

Dropping the reins to this old horse
her body bears its necessities alone.
The grass lives through patches of dirt to fine dust.
Through old cars and childhood tracks
she pushes with her shoulders against blades
and seeds of narrowness. Insubstantial, the meek do not intrude.
Numb aperture, the blind eye of the horse
that turns eighteen years into a wild combustion
of cheat grass. Dust enters dust.
Grief drifts through remnants of another form.
Weeds tumbling over potato fields
weave into the barbed wire fence—our blanket of thorn and rust.
Clouds. Hills are brightness.
In its solitary position between breasts and field,
her heart moves to acceptance
of a ride on an old horse.
Belly shivers and haunches flinch.
Collecting dust the body bears silence well.

WE REMEMBER OUR RELATIVES

We begin with flowers beaded onto the cradleboard.
The mattress and forms hold the child's head center and upright:
The legs and spine will be straight.
The laces spiral over the center: They will shape the child.
The baby emerges from the womb and is safely enclosed again.
Leaning on a tree or hanging from a saddle,
the child is connected to us and watches as we gather
huckleberries, catch and clean salmon, dry the roots.
This beginning with protection is brilliant
with attention to detail: cradleboards have a song.
Shells tinkle on the rounded rose bough
that guards the child's face as we walk.
Contoured flowers edging the carriage in arms,
made by relatives especially for the child
to ensure the soul will bloom.

WEAVING

for Margaret Jim-Pennah and Gladys McDonald

Weaving baskets you twine the strands into four parts.
Then, another four. The four directions many times.
Pairs of fibers spiral around smaller and smaller sets of threads.
Then, one each time. Spirals hold all this design
airtight and pure. This is our house, over and over.
Our little sisters, Khoush, Sowitk, Piaxi, Wakamu,
the roots will rest inside.
We will be together in this basket.
We will be together in this life.

SHELLS ON STONE

We left shells on stone.
My family's hands move to release shells.
The memory of origin.
We wear these elements at necessary times for strength.
We remember how helpless we were, leaving our beginning.
Not knowing, not expecting our tasks
to be part of immense concentric rings.
Water is always present.
The salmon in the season of warm winds.
The roots in spring.
Huckleberries, deep colored and round,
roll into exquisite baskets with mountain designs.
The fir boughs cover the berries for coolness and fragrance.
The red choke cherries hang as if heavy with snow,
bittersweet to the tongue.
The deer walks quietly in our lives.
The elk, heavy with challenge, whistles,
his horns bent back over his rich brown shoulders.
Our bodies contain all of these rings and motion.

LONGHOUSE I

The circle is made of ourselves.
Relatives, friends linger past the comfort of age and sleep.
The people are a circle of respect on the floor.
East is the sun, a pattern painted over the door frame.
Songs gather in motion, in the rustle of drummers.
Seven hearts. Seven pairs of hands. Seven parts of the earth.
The rumble calls into the echo, the longhouse of our past.
In this house shawls rest over shoulders like palms.
In this house children in simple lines move around the floor.
Oldest to smallest, the floor vibrates with the dancers.
A song in one throat draws up the drums.
The hand moves. With one heart, we move.
The song is in each place, seen and unseen.
Shells move as feathers touch air.
We send this pulse to the center and outward.
The sun over our heads extends hands of warmth.
We send out a surge of recognition with one light.

LONGHOUSE II

My great-uncle and his nephews kneel together.
Heads bent, right hands cupped and swing
arcing to the center of chests.
They move from knees to feet in a simple and smooth lift.
This is our sight. As men dance,
they are beads in the string of song

My great-aunt stands face to the center,
her daughters and nieces beside her.
They cup their hands like everyone around them,
walk the circle, twirling, hands raised at West, then East.
Their skirts wave in grace There is energy as this is made
of light and our blood. Our mind's wind moves among us.

Their voices are pure, tell of our timeless choice.
Lines of hearts filling, voices spark a warmth
into the bleak cavity held too long in the weary.
Knees bend and lift to join with threads
of brilliant hairpipe bones and shell necklaces.
The beat of skin upon skin. Seven times. Sets of seven.

SISTERS?

Sister-girl's boyfriend was a country gentleman. A cowboy
with polished boots, pressed western shirts, bootcut jeans.
He used to visit every year for his proposal.
"Marry me before we run out of water."
"Marry me before we have too much trouble, run out of food."
She always refused and dated him anyway.
Once they went to the Disco-a-Go-Go.
By polite mistake, he accepted a dance
with a woman who was really a man.
Sister-girl said, to prove it, "Look at her big feet!"
She was jealous. He was amazed.
Later, when they went to a movie,
the ticket taker asked, "Sisters?"
He said, "*No!* I'm her boyfriend!"
He was sensitive about his long, traditional braids.
Straight people in the seventies made rude comments
about long hair on men.
Sister-girl giggled, "Honey, that's the name of the movie."
He was sweet and rarely allowed himself the privilege of anger.
He believed in Peace and Love,
but not the movement-of-the-time's kind.
Years later he was found dead in a laundromat.
He had never married.

SISTERS

"Is that your daughter?" strangers asked.
I looked sixteen when I turned twelve.
My sister was always small.
Now she is five feet tall and shaped like both her grandmothers.
She would melt against my side, under my arm.
Sometimes she slept this way.
I watched her like a *nana* is supposed to.
Once, while I held her cradleboard,
waiting in the Women's Park in Portland,
people smiled at us.
I lifted her blanket from the bough
to admire her. Somehow, she had wiggled
out of her lacings.
She was hanging upside down like a bat,
sleeping soundly. I put her back.
That was the start of all the times I would save her life,
upside down.
When she slipped under a log at Shitike Creek and almost
drowned.
When she swallowed a dime. It rolled out of her mouth
across the floor as I held her feet and hit between her shoulders.
The other times were right side up.
The house fire. Teenage hysteria. Loneliness. Laughter.
I held her shoulders, wrestling with her strength.
Calmly, our mother predicts that our separate
struggles will not hold us apart.

SPEELYAY THOUGHTS IN SEATTLE

Riding an elevator, my aunties and I, dressed
in fine city clothes, go up in an empty building. Go down.
Talking, laughing, we hear the echo of our happiness.
One aunt says, "This must be how the Huckleberry Sisters feel.
Inside Coyote's belly, talking of how things go right. Go wrong
when no one listens."
Go up. Go down in the vacuous interior of Speelyay.
Inside the big building, Speelyay jokes with us.
Our laughter is louder as we reach the ground floor.
We laugh about Speelyay, the original one.
He never seemed to recall being given advice from the sisters.
He thought the words just came to him: *Ki-yay ki-yay!*
How to outwit myself…self-troubled foolishness and slapstick.
Headstrong Coyote never listened to anyone,
except to hear himself talk.

SPEELYAY, AGAIN!

Riding another elevator, in another building,
my mother and I stand side by side.
Head to toe, similar height, face and wavy hair.
On the eighth floor the door opens.
A woman stops and looks at each of us, asks, "Sisters?"
as the door closes on her question and amazement.
We laugh, arrive at the doctor's office on the sixteenth floor.
They heard our laughter ascend from the eighth.
Everyone is smiling. The receptionist says,
"Laughter is the best medicine."
Laughter *is* the best *medicine!*
Coyote thinks so, as he laughs too much.
He farts obnoxiously loud too.
He has an earthy attitude.
He watches people, separate from their bodies,
posturing with polite manners.
Pressure builds in the belly.
Where can it go?

COYOTE FOLKLORE,
IN IMAGE AND PRACTICE

At the Institute of American Indian Arts a professor
famous for his relationship with Coyote
pulls two eyeballs from his pocket.
Plastic, with one blue and one green iris, they wiggle on his palm.
The assembled artists and poets look
at his out-of-pocket treasures. Someone yells, Coyote!
The holder of the eyeballs is very clever.
He leans back with a smile, successful with his surprise.
For those who know how Coyote always fooled
with his body parts, Coyote appears.
Oblivious to this allusion, this is the painter's
most perfect performance.

Two of us recall that Coyote had to put flowers
in his empty sockets to chase the bird who stole his eyes.
(The famous painter puts the eyeballs back into his pocket.)
Coyote was juggling them for fun. The bird took his playthings.
Then everyone had fun with them. One of us says,
"This story is long and variable. We can't tell a complete tale
except in winter." Like Coyote foiled, the man
with the extra pair of eyes ignores us and walks away.

Upon hearing this story in the Northwest, an artist chuckles,
knowing the full lascivious version, "I was reading about Coyote
and his eyeballs just the other day!"
Later a sculptor tells me, "That's the most pleasant image
of Coyote, with flowers for eyes." She smiles
as she pats the nose of a clay Coyote with affection.
"I thought everyone knew about it."

DISTANT COUSINS

Our mothers were best friends.
Our grandmothers were best friends.
We had little choice.
We sat on opposite sides of our small table,
legs crossed, plates in front of us.
We had deer liver, potatoes and broken ears of corn.
My cousin sat up tall, eyes fierce, sounding like someone else.
"I am a Nez Perce. The best people on earth!" she declared.
"You are a low down, good for nothing!"
Shocked, I threw my buttered corn cob in her face.
The waste of precious food put her off center.
I leaped over the table and pushed her back.
We rolled over the floor and out the open door.
She screamed for our grandmother who was watering
the lawn with her thumb over the hose end.
We jockeyed for position:
"Granma, she's beating me up!"
"Granma, she called me a good for nothing!"
She sprayed us with water and scolded,
"For god's sake, if you are going to act like mad dogs,
I'll treat you like that, too."
Much later, we watched adults play out the same feral struggle,
without the benefit of a wise leader.

DEER!

Deer Sister, Deer Mother, Deer Father, Deer Aunty, Deer Uncle.
Deer Uncle, as he approaches a bend in the mountain road
at night, emphatically whispers, "Deer!" to his children.
They slow and round the turn. A deer is standing there, waiting.

When Deer Grandmother claps her hands in the car, saying,
"Deer!" Deer!" Deer Grandfather answers, "What, honey?"
She hits his shoulder, "Not you! Deer are coming!"
They roll down the hill and deer appear at the edge of the road.

Going to the meeting and joining of three rivers,
Deschutes, Metolius and the Crooked River, we stop.
Shyly, my friend and I walk up to a doe
who stands in the road, waiting.
She is patient and blows her breath on our palms.
Her nose is soft and moist. It feels like nothing
when we touch it. "My grandfather had a deer named Blossom,"
I tell my friend. "She danced in the Fourth of July parade
with their matching palominos. She always wore a bell
on a red ribbon around her neck. Jealousy eventually killed her."

CHINLE SUMMER

Loneliness for me is being a daughter of two landscapes,
distant from the horizon circling me.
The red earth completely round.
The sky a deep bowl of turquoise overhead.
Mother and father. Loneliness
rising up like thunderheads. The rain pours over
the smooth rocks into the canyon that is familiar.

This is the road that leads to my father's home.
After twenty years I stand on the threshold of his mother's hogan.
Grandmother sits in the cool dark, out of the light
from the door and smoke hole. She talks softly
in the Diné language.

Talking to me as I grew in her warmth, my mother
lowered herself into this canyon, barefoot and unafraid.
She walked miles in high heels to church by this road
that runs alongside Canyon de Chelly.
She was a river woman walking in dust.

The Recumbent Woman whispers inside different languages.
I am one story. Beauty walked South then North again.
Beauty sparked physical creation.

A strong and wild will draws up the land into the body.
My journey circles back, unraveling, remaking itself
like the magnificent loom work of my grandmother's center.
My grandfather once told me, "Lizzy, I was busy singing
over there…you were here. So, I came home to see you."

UNITY

Summer

Night's heat in high desert moves into the cricket's legs.
I have eyes that are brown cattails,
still and dry as the copper urn.
The heat is touching fireweeds
along the trail home. Smooth, light-green bark
on river willow mingles in the scent of another memory.
Along the creek below, willow and cottonwood
rise from moisture and the valley's age.

Fall

Blue offerings on my canvas edge out from another corner.
Colors linger on capped, blank indecisions
of paint tubes. Curled ribs bend from the palette.
There is in this cooling remembrance, an auditory fall,
as red and gold spaces in passing leaves roll and lap
at the paved road. The purr in rain paints windows.
Moist breath collects on the interior pane,
becoming a mask for the woman who stands behind it.

Winter

Beads string into silence. Light waves within the wind.
Outside, trees move against the bones of this house.
Shadows cloud and project into the blackened fireplace.
Alternatively cold and warm, brightness edges center, picking

at pieces of patterned decoration in the linoleum.
The dip of my back begins to feel the pressure of desire.
I shape small glass beads into family patterns:
the stained glass of mission churches
and the wildflowers graceful curl on buckskin

Our Spring

Hands lift under the sheets in changing arrangements.
A distant face rises over sharp outlines of junipers
and lingering brush of sage. Curtains whisper.
Weaving, wind sweeps and leaves the sill smooth
as burnished basalt in the moon's arousal.
Personal clutter, tumbled onto the floor, illustrates
our separation. We move as stars that twirl outward.
Without edge, prayers as lips move together.
In our flesh, we gather in our separate sorrows,
notes of tension and distances. Commotion holds
the center of mouths, not speaking or telling
which direction the weather moves. We cannot say
what we will need as we dress in the morning for experience.

Summer

I dodge a small dusty whirlwind.
Secretly, I see my shadow match its funnel.
Vicariously, it touches my fortune.
Winding parachutes of dandelions overtake with peace
lightness in space. Solitude in the house
pierces itself with settlement of gravity.
The floorboards creak in despondent parts.

A polish of warm and vibrant yellows spreads
the sun over hillsides. Blue moon and night

turn inside folds of shifting reason.
The new flowers, small wild roses and thorns,
late buds and protection have grown without attention.
Sturdy gentleness forms pearls that emerge in this country,
one and one. I will braid single buds into my hair.
Beside the river, many summers ago, I had sage
in these strands, sleeping in a comfortable hollow
beside the smooth, quiet smells of the river.

III

HAND INTO STONE

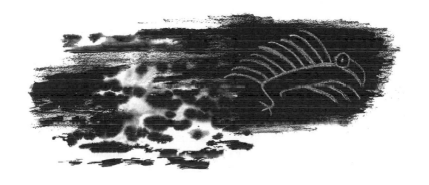

WYAM: ECHO OF FALLING WATER

FOR MORE THAN twelve thousand years, Wyam (Celilo Falls) was an important trade center on the Chewana (Columbia River)—part of a network that extended from California to Alaska, as far east as Missouri, and eventually west to Hawaii. The civilizations of the Northwest that preceded the advent of the Euro-Americans, Asian-Americans, Polynesian-Americans, and African-Americans were sustained by an elaborate societal structure of individual cultures and sovereign governments. It has been described by the leaders at Warm Springs as a system embodied by the phrase *tee-cha-meengsh-mee sin-wit nu-me ud-wu-la-man-wil*. (At the time of creation the Creator placed us in this land and gave us the voice of this land and that is our law.)

These unwritten laws sustained the environment and its people to ensure the renewal of abundance, especially the seasonal return of the spawning salmon, the *nusoox*. The fishing and extensive trade routes along the river and its tributaries created a cultural bounty which the newcomers, also, were welcome to share, in order to sustain themselves.

Wyam was the pivotal trade center of the Sahaptin-speaking people (Yakama, Umatilla, Walla Walla, Warm Springs, Wanapums, Wyampums, and others) and the Wasco/Chinookan-speaking people. "Great Rendezvous" would occur at Wyam, where wealth was exchanged and alliances formed. Marriages were arranged, betrothal ceremonies performed, horses traded and raced, gambling—such as stick games—was enjoyed, and families were reunited. It was also here that information was exchanged and passed along: news from across the continent, the announcement of Lewis and Clark's arrival in the Northwest, tribal news, and gossip.

For the Wyampums and Warm Springs people, Wyam was not only a trade and communication center, it was also the heart of their daily lives. Here were the most significant fisheries along the Middle Columbia River, with fishing sites passed along only through inheritance. Fishing (dip netting) was done from immense platforms built above the white water on the "fishing rocks" above the falls. The first salmon of the season was honored by ceremony, and a salmon feast was held to give thanks for the return of the salmon.

Salmon was a key element in the spiritual framework of my people: purity of foods, purity of thought, purity of body. It was part of the litany of praise to those things without which life wouldn't be possible (which also included the deer, the roots, the berries, the sun, the earth, and the water). The entire fish was used, except for the guts. Nothing was wasted. Packed with vitamins, beneficial oils, and minerals—fresh or dried—it was nearly complete nutritionally. Massive amounts of salmon were stored over the winter, and the excess was traded for specialty items. Abundant salmon runs ensured that anyone willing to work wouldn't starve.

Wyam—the longest continuously inhabited site of human habitation in the Northwest, possibly in the U.S.—was destroyed by the U.S. Army Corps of Engineers on March 10, 1957, when the massive steel and concrete gates of The Dalles Dam closed and choked the downstream surge of the Columbia River. Six hours later and eight miles upstream, Wyam, the age-old fisheries and falls, was under water and lost forever.[1]

Shortly before The Dalles Dam was opened, the U.S. Army Corps of Engineers met with leaders from Yakama, Warm Springs, Umatilla, and Nez Perce and a settlement was reached. Wyampum's chief, Tommy Thompson, who was still living at

Celilo Village, refused to "signature his salmon away" and instead held a prayer and song ceremony exhorting Congress to vote against the dam's opening. Chief Thompson said, "The Almighty took a long time to make this place." An eloquent leader, who possessed a spiritual integrity like so many great leaders of the area, he was one of many who still revered the ancient lifeways given to the people by the Creator at the time of creation. He taught (by example) respect for the natural laws tribes adhered to, which ensured that no more was taken than needed and that the rest continued to grow and proliferate.

The dam destroyed major fishing sites reserved by the Plateau people of the Middle Columbia River in the Treaty of 1855. Although the tribes were compensated for the loss of the fisheries at Celilo Falls, the United States has never fulfilled its responsibility, pursuant to the agreement, to jointly with the tribal governments assign in-lieu sites for Native fishermen along the river.

Despite the absence of "in lieu sites," people still needed to fish. David Sohappy was one of those who continued to fish and live along the river as the Creator intended, honoring the salmon and the traditional foods on a daily basis. He was one of many Yakama leaders to file suit in order to seek definition of treaty rights on the river and to determine to what extent state agencies could regulate Indian fishing. After many long years in the courts, Judge Belloni's ruling in the combined case *Sohappy vs. Smith/U.S. vs. Oregon* enabled the tribes to achieve greater participation in contemporary resource management with the states. So far, there have been seven U.S. Supreme Court decisions upholding the 1855 treaty guaranteeing to the Columbia River indigenous people the traditional right to harvest the salmon. This includes the right to conduct religious ceremonies for the renewal of the salmon.

Although the political climate of the seventies and eighties gave support to Native Americans exercising their treaty rights, the fishing rights cases exacerbated the underlying political and racial tensions of the region. Those who maintained a presence in our traditional homelands became the focus of state and federal agencies to whom tourism and commercial fishing were more important than honoring Native American treaty rights or the hardships of the Native American citizens and natural ecosystems. In 1982, as a result of his activism, David Sohappy was targeted in a fourteen-month undercover operation referred to as "Salmon Scam," and sentenced to five years in prison for selling 317 "illegal" fish to agents. (At this same time, dozens of non–Native American commercial fishermen were the subject of investigation but none were imprisoned for their "illegal" catch.) David Sohappy had hoped that his resistance would become a catalyst for reassertion of indigenous presence along the river, since it was covered extensively by the media. He served twenty-two months in federal prison and suffered a series of strokes during his incarceration. He was released in May of 1988 but still faced seven and a half years of federal probation.[2] Shortly afterward, David Sohappy died at sixty-six years of age on May 7, 1991. His position is best stated in his 1988 statement to the U.S. Senate Select Committee on Indian Affairs, where he explained, "I am a Wanapum, a river person, and I belong on the banks of the Chewana. If I can honor the salmon in our traditional manner, the Creator has promised to return it one-thousand fold. The non-Indian regulations have failed. Why should they still keep telling me not to fish? My life is for the salmon, after my work is done, I will move on."

During all this time and still today few understand the political-cultural-spiritual lifeway that, at its core, concerned itself with the return of the salmon and the health of the ecosystem, the great river system that enabled the salmon to proliferate in large numbers. Similarly, few non–Native Americans understand that our sovereignty as a people was not bestowed upon us by the U.S. government or its treaties. *Ne-shy-chus* is the word that expresses the fact of our *innate* sovereignty—indigenous people, such as the Warm Springs people, are rooted in ancestral domain, free of any outside forces. The 1855 treaty between the ancient governments of the

Columbia Plateau and the infant United States government does not represent the granting of "special privileges" but is a recognition of rights that are prior and inextinguishable, rights reserved to the tribes by virtue of prior legal claims as first citizens of this land. Tribal members have dual citizenship. We participate in two governments: our tribal government and the U.S. government. Each individual possesses a voice and a vote for both, though tribal members did not hold U.S. citizenship until 1924.

The Pacific Northwest is renowned for its natural beauty and livability, but the riches of our homeland are being spent without conscience or regard for its long history or its people.[3] The tribes had always maintained an internal system of checks and balances for maintenance and harvest. We honored the natural laws of the earth, its physical requirements. We followed cultural and spiritual systems and worked collaboratively through an ancient, nondestructive process to promote health and prosperity for the land, families, and nonhuman beings that live here. This practice was handed down from one generation to the next, in home life, work, community, and the longhouse.

The unconscionable drowning of Wyam—Celilo Falls—marks a crucial point in our collective history. It destroyed a major cultural site and rent a multi-millennial relationship of a people to a place. After nearly four decades, Celilo Falls is still talked about and remembered as the heart of our homeland. It was like a mother, nourishing us, and is remembered as a place of great peace.

1. The Dalles Dam is one of twenty large hydroelectric dams built in the mainstream Columbia River since 1910. These blockages began the decline of salmon runs and spawning grounds that would be accelerated in the decades to come by industrial and agricultural pollution, rampant commercial ocean harvesting, and clear cutting. Before 1855, approximately fourteen million salmon and steelhead swam up the Columbia River. A hundred and forty years later an estimated two and a half million return has added two species to the endangered species list of 1994.

2. I believe that it was also as a result of his activism that David Sohappy and his family received a notice of eviction from their home at Cook's Landing.

3. The Chewana is being polluted with toxic wastes and discharges from aluminum and nuclear facilities; it is currently the most polluted and radioactive waterway in the world. The recent release of information from the Department of Energy about radioactive waste materials being released and "experiments" with radiation upon the river, salmon and people, documents a tragedy of immense proportions.

She Walks along the River

IN MEMORY OF CROSSING THE COLUMBIA

For Charlotte Edwards Pitt and Charlotte Agnes Pitt

My board and blanket were Navajo,
but my bed is inside the river.
In the beads of remembrance,
I am her body in my father's hands.
She gave me her eyes
and the warmth of basalt.
The vertebrae of her back,
my breastplate, the sturdy
belly of mountainside.

"Pahtu," he whispered in her language.
She is the mountain of change.
She is the mountain of women
who have lain as volcanoes
before men.

Red, as the woman much loved,
she twisted like silvery Chinook
beyond his reach.

Dancing the Woman-Salmon dance,
there is not much time to waste.

BLACK NIGHT STONES AND
THE SHINE OF ABALONE

We are spiders making our beds
within a horseshoe of sage,
inside the river of smell.

In Klickitat basket designs,
volcanic ridges crumble by the half
moon as speckled rocks.

With a persistence
the sound of heat,
its small mysteries of insects
rattle against the round moon and sky.

Stars sear the face of constellations,
the Great Bear, the Seven Brothers
of the dipper,
and the mythic Grandmothers trail tiny dogs behind them.

Trees restrain their birds,
hold their callused feet.
As thighs they brace
the long strain of hillside.

The old ridges of our parents' hands,
like warm, moist clay,
press over us as we begin to sleep.

In the dark shells of our dreaming
wild roses, bullheads
and pungent junipers shake around us.

The river currents her back
over the small, black stones,
a tongue of Wasco sounds.

The medicine people sing,
a language rumbles in the throat
of knowledge.

With medicine in their hands
and abalone eyes, they wave eagle feathers
over our ailments and silent prayers.

HAND INTO STONE

Someday the land will be our eyes and skin again.
—My grandmother, Elizabeth Pitt, at seventy-five

Her creped fingers,
teeth marked with red speckles,
held mine tight
as she showed our finger moons to me.
They grew together as snowy stones
scratching themselves sleepily.

She had long fingers
with the mobility of spiders.
I felt them at night
as they climbed my skin.
She wrapped us
in tight shells
with agate crystals.

We breathed in our own breath
under this cover.

OF STEPS TO DROWNING

The pain of empty flower stems
held the few hairs,
the brightness
that must be recaptured.
Disappearing as strings
of romance, they are resonant as tight bow
for selected deer.

They wish to wander
under current with lost need
and fly in moss with conifers.

They hold little stars of dew
in lack of other possessions or petals
for charm, peer into faces
to destination and last mourn.

Hands, burnt bone and dusty,
offer rain caches of gems.
Moving in sign talk for swollen eyes
they reach for voice
to the open cave and rushes of silent bats.
They disappear with small wings.

Beside scented chants
the meadowlark dips vocal
with river and crisp grass.

The wishes reach for gifts
to wandering hair, but are armless
to rub these blind, folded eyes.

As a new buck in itchy velvet,
one rubs to the skin translucent,
tight against the receptacles of light.
The irises are of nights dreaming.

The losses are small sounds of moaning.
Bead necklaces of stone and shell
slide into the world of minnows.
Bones grasp at mosses and branch
to muddy the water for drowning.

SHE-WHO-WATCHES, THE NAMES ARE PRAYER

For David Sohappy, April 25, 1925 – May 7, 1991

My humanness is an embellished tongue,
the bell, a yellow mouth of September's
moon beats outward. She speaks for all
the names that clang in memorial.

There is Celilo,
dispossessed, the village of neglect
and bad structure.
The falls are faint rocks enrippled
in the placid lake of back waters.
With a sad, stone grief and wisdom
I overlook the railroad.
The tight bands rail along
the whirls of the Columbia.
Drowning is a sensation
fishermen and their wives know of.
Men who fished son after father.
There are drownings in The Dalles,
hanging in jails and off-reservation suicide-towns.

A strange land awaits
the fishermen,
as it had for the Nez Perce, the Navajo, the Cheyenne,
those who wailed in the Long Walks,
keened open the graves of their families.
The dead children.
My children,
with names handed down and unused.

Nee Mee Poo, Diné, Tsistsistas.
The people, pure in emergence.
The immense mother is crying.
"Human beings,"
the words are tremors in the rib cage
of hills.

The consumption of loneliness binds us.
Children lie on the railroad tracks
to die from the wail of night and spirits.
I watch for the rushing head of chaos
and flat hands grope from the cattle cars,
clamor in the swift, fresh air.
A sky is clicking through the regular slats.
The tail whips the dusty battles of the Indian Wars,
unsettling itself, nude and raw.
Celilo Falls sank unwillingly in the new trading
and everyone dissolved in the fall.

THE SENSE

Obliterate your conscious light and you will see.

It is liniment
of brain colored slip
for tables of mosaic premonitions.
Faint oracles
thin and weave filaments of hair.

It is an inner layer
of fine, quivering skin,
escalating
through millennia over millennia,
sucking inner organs,
shedding dormant cells.

You hear the forest topsoil
gestate then chew itself.
It mimics you as a bird
undulating your bird neck.

ORIGINATING FIRE

For the communities near the Hanford Nuclear Reservation.

A barren thief scratches at the door
and dims the moon, the candle
to answer inferior medicines.
That empty spirit haunts our origins,
tapping our likeness into conformity.

Light on the skyline is First Fire
never leaving its journey, waiting.
There is movement of foreign substance
rumbling bones into tufaceous soil.

Boulders and tule huts move without light and sound
away from the impressions basalt formed in the wake
of smoke. Blown into the grunts of animal.
Children sleep through the nightmare,
where the uncontrolled fire
is imprisoned light.

BLACK FEAR

Pointing, his face looked at the blackened windows.
The boat was stripped of shine,
old and blackened with paint.
Electrical tape on chrome.
"Renegades," worded itself in his mind.

Explanation of renegades are hinted,
never known fully, until
you are blackened in the act, in night,
libeled as illegal fishermen.

Dark tread in water,
on watch in pitch black.
Sleeping on fish scales.
Fish, eye to eye,
no engine, oars lapping the nets in.
Fear, in the darkness, the river's depths undone.

The river's depths undone into fishermen's nets,
moistly tickling their backs.
Unwound like an Indian woman's hair,
full and soft down her back,
touching the hungry child in bed.

The fear is to find dark hair clinging
to silver scaled on the sides of a fish.
The fear is to see the police trespass

on other people's land to break
the Indian renegade's fingers,
leaving the hard callused work
in those hands, useless and dark.

SHAKER CHURCH PRAYER

Her feet raise dust.
Shaker songs
stomp, stomp,
crack the floorboards.

Pairs of bells,
round, brass mountains
erupt from their hands.

They rise for calls of prayer.
Throw the evil away.
Bring the light in.

Ears ring and numb.
Candle flames suspend
the shape of Jesus' cross.

She sways, the song and breath
is expelled through the tight lips.

Hands draw
up Grandmother's sore posture.

The candles above them are brilliant.
The bells crack.
Our floor erupts with feet.

She knows how to heal.
Her eyes are closed
and she sees the source of disease.

They rise in the prayer.
Throw the evil away.
Bring the light in.

Her hands tremble from the wrist,
hold off the darkness.

Arms embrace with the light and air
of song and prayer.

The church trembles,
then we rest.

BIRDS IN THIS WOMAN

For Lillian Pitt, mask-maker

The Eavesdropper

In her yard they feed
at the cylinder of seed
under her awning.
The birds sift
through the groves of junipers
that grasp and shudder
juices from their deep root.

They gossip, especially the black
and white magpie.
They steal words from people.
Raspy tales, choked
out without much attention
as to what is true
and what is lie.

They are mostly black
accentuated with white.
She is careful of her words near this quick-tongued
gossip robber.

Feathers

In the clayish dirt she finds a feather,
then another, pockets them
with the bundle of wings,
bluejay tail, fluffs.

Lost in wind she collects feathers.
Later at distance,
they will be planted.
She does not hoard gifts.
They are experiences.

Ravens

She asked two ravens
for feathers.
They winged over the apple trees
and left two feathers
in the grass.

It is peculiar,
they do not shine.
They are not true black
but all blacks
fired into one another.
They dangle from the wall.
She visits ravens, maybe once
every week. Cawing, they are big
for birds, when one must eat
many times its own weight
to fly.

She saw a lifeless raven
impaled on a branch, empty
eyed, ruffled.
He is a bird nested in ill wind.
Perhaps victim of the wind's secrets
that night hides. It was violence,
horribly corrupted magic
that killed that bird,
winged into crucifixion.

Hair raised on the nape
of her neck, she hurried to the river
to soak her face and cool the anger
and impulse of her hair.

The Gentle Bird

As a young girl, she had a small, black bird.
Unable to fly, it was carried on her shoulders.
At Pi-Ume-Sha, she talked with a woman called Bird.
Bird said, "Be careful with this bird.
They are delicate and hungry."
Bird is a singer, she listened to her songs.
She stood there all day, shaded
the bird from June sun
and watched the feathers swing on the dancers.
She does not remember where her bird went,
only that it seemed gentle.
It scratched the dry grass
in its box, impatient for her.

How the Hawk Lives

There is a hawk that lives
at our old ranch house
in Tenino Valley.
She kees, has a rough nest
that grows each year in the poplars.
It was here that she found a gray kitten.
Fighting with the screech hawk
she rescued her.
Her side had hawk marks.
She fit in the hand
and became a strong cat,

one-eyed and lithe,
protecting the house from spiders, snakes
and mice. No birds.
She allows the magpies to eat her food.
Only the dog chases them.
She is a bird dog.

Gifts

To rid themselves of ache,
mental and ones of the body,
she bathed in the hot springs with her mother.
They inhaled the sulfurous smell
deep to keep as a remembrance,
for when it would become necessary to be healed again.

Feathers appear everywhere.
When she walks, feathers
are before her step.
She collects them all.
Even when she stops by the window
they fall past in spirals,
no bird in sight.
She lets them fall, it is enough
to remind her of birds.

There was that time she rode
from Wapnitia to Simnasho
with her mother and grandmother,
a brown, staring eagle flew beside them,
looking at each one carefully.
Grandmother smiled, "This is a blessing."

Whisper of Wings

Yellowhawk told of trees,
how they speak from their roots,
she hears it. It is undeniable.
Listen.
In her yard, birds chatter,
bustle together, consumed
in the old effort of gathering.
In a flight of circles, they migrate.

As witness, she makes birds,
makes animals and people who wear these feathers.
They have rushes and fibers sing from their mouths.
She pulls the feathers
from her bundle and places them,
liking the feel of wind
resisting the curving spines.

Winter boughs add needles
incant, "Birds—there are so many birds,"
as they whisper over wings.

SPIDER WOMAN'S COYOTE BONES

Coyote didn't do anything. It was already here for him when he got here.
    —My grandmother, Elizabeth Pitt, at seventy-nine

I will speak plainly.
That is how I speak, past the skin,
through the teeth.

It is the same house here,
same woman, same dress
of intangible material.
My grandmother made this,
her mother also.
We are the same woman.
Not dead.

Women believed your Coyote falsehoods.
I come back to catch you
in your glamorous animal skins,
the changes of tint
each time you are glimpsed.
I gaze to the bones.
You know I am back.
You have shed and left.

Tired, you shifted through the phases
of false power.
In the carcass of your wiles
I shake the flies away—the crows.
I poke my finger into the holes
of what you acquired by seduction.

Your lips talk against yourself,
thin into mirages.

This dark face is intent.
I live by observations, agility.
Not material,
I reverently travel space.
Every beaded Dreamer bag you pack
is made by an Indian woman.
We bead and endure.
We give it away.
When you are a maker, you make symbols of yourself.
Look at the fine work and see what is left
from massacre.

We have died.
It is evidence of faith to create.

I am alive past tradition.
I am stronger without grandeur.
In my own bed of legs and blood,
I am sustained from the food collected
with my hands.
I live in the house that I create,
create, create,
work until it stands right here.
No fantasy.
I made it. You were given the form.
Before us, that is how it was.

I have that memory.
That silky whisper in my ears
from these threads.
You pick things for collection,

not as absolution from your buffoonery.
Do not fight me.
I have been a target
for generations.
I have stood in front of fatal moments
repeatedly.

"When the dance is over, Sweetheart…"
and you fold away your regalia,
you will sense my sweat all over your body,
over your nerves.
This is not unpleasant,
you looked fine.
I talked this into existence.
And as you have said,
"Your tongue does wonderful things besides speak."

I warned that you would tire your legs
satisfying this itch.
I think of this as my throat constricts.
I have said enough.
There is no myth,
only prophecy is left.

She Walks across the Country

SCRATCH MEDICINE AND TENEMENTS

In this house the regal apparition
is the headdress on the bureau,
a reminder of well-dressed whims.
Your wing is in place beside the bird,
content on the escape outside,
a restful pose of enacted circles.

The flight northward, the wish southward.
Between the breasts is a silver star
haloing circumferences,
a hot arm, bite of old aches
and simulated lines of fortune on the palms.
This is the warm moist place of eyes
in the heart, quick and squinting in light
too harsh for night cats.

The door is broken again from drunks
bursting forth and inward.
Splattered with acid, the walls evidence
batteries and disintegration.

My edgeful certainty is marked boundaries of graffiti.
Spiraled laments of tomcats, heads ripped of ears,
nestles into this house of delirium.
With hairs between the fingers and tastes of brine,
old hides and horse breath under a sad tongue,
there is a gasp of air, a fast ride over stoniness.

The tremble of prediction is recovery of the past,
not a past, but the burning of old houses,
tar-papered shacks and poisoned blankets laced
with small pox.

Our hair touches in the dirt
and has remained that way as thoughts.
Evocative night calls, birds
in the shimmer of naked trees
push against the slant of winter and drought.

Without this peace, there is the scratch
of the lost stray,
the wildcat of hard-bitten tidbits of remedy.
The only way back is by the direction formed
in the flowering strips of Grandmother's dress
encircling our limbs.

SIAMESE GHOSTS (THE DISTURBED SPIRITS)

The clouds were nuclear mushrooms
suspended over pastures
We watched the fallout as dull
scales grimaced in many follicles
Birds in the aviaries unknowingly
wed laying eggs in the shape
of spider bodies
They crumbled beneath their bellies
into hollow bone
the shards of our skulls rolled maniacally
as delicate bells

We knew ourselves
as clouds and rain
of some ocean quality

Our shine bent
in prisms
(the eyes)
Our sight
beat as moths
(the eyelashes)
Our anemone grew
tangled and long
(the hands)
into slender octopuses
who search and fight beak to beak
into a curl

a spurt of ink
Confusion met the next man
desirous of sinners

A damned man for the attended graves
he grasps the collapsible mess
while we move our soft heads to refuge
Endowed with our detachable arms
he finds an oasis

In the desert we watched
the dunes grow
until we couldn't climb only look
as we moved around and past
when we could be home
be little girls in daddy arms
little twinkles in his iris
For encore we search
the familiar gestures
As some alien we imagine
to feel the first night
we closed our eyes in sleep
Alone
without the other heartbeat
back in the darkness
and liquid visions
of sounds and wavelength

Nurtured by silent vigilance
we held the mysterious forms
the search
for this earthly mirage of insanity
Abrasions scabbed
on our skin

as visual deformity
We were always clairvoyant
formed for the cavity
to hold another
set of androids
or blind albino fish
we dug out of the depths

Somewhere
in the jet black
we had forgotten
what we felt   The swelled
energy of attraction
bent the trees
as if in the hurricane
a tunnel of livid leaves
The serenity made others
hungry to devour
us as some Japanese dish
with the kimonos
and carp cutouts
glued as kites
The sewer smell of humanity
deterred us
from the final ceremony
the quiet teahouse
simple perfect art
the slender knife
for our white sides to ingest
The inexplicability
put us in a child's notebook
"Yes, they are crazy"
some busy mother said

comfortably between
each dish on the rack.

A tear caught on the blade
of grass said it well
reflective of blue
our skycaps
and two black dots
of babies we lost
The blood harps
in manifest transparency
The rage of red seed
called for a father
the hanged man
to return
and order them
back in   to the womb
Cells in stopped division
were dead fetuses
That didn't hurt as much
as cryptic rejection   we read
in the black-eyed   stare
of the ceiling

Demerits
we felt as diamond chips
in our stomachs let
that black specter enter
as a man would
First me then you
and tear the wombs
into burst balloons
the shreds into execution walls

"Never again"
I said to you
We knew the miracle of death
and we weren't good
enough to condemn ourselves
in confessional
innocence

Downstairs
we felt the lock break
from the gallows
and colors fled
as cancer
into our beloved
ones   the anchors
We beat the sides
trying to calm the sea
and ate the charm
of a dragonfly
The heart was
some incessant
hammer at blank
boards and plank
making nothing except Arctic
night   for months we groped
in darkness   Night wore
our nerves as bangles
so we changed the colors
in the TV
and made purple
pink lips on blonde
women and puppets
out of analysts

It was the sequel
to Punch and Judy
that scared us out
into circular night drives
We forced the moon
to wed water
The waves churned
It bit our ears as cold wind
taunted us as tides

When we joined the baby
shockers in the city of holy faith
we danced to heavy violence
You moved your arms
in secret choreography
I ground my hips
until the joints
squealed out my fullish lips
The laughter hurt our faces
but we hadn't stopped since
childhood
It was our late
We left the town
unfound
unformed
just bounces of external forces
light beams
and city stars

We carved out monuments
as night girls
They called us on anonymous phones
and walked

symbolically
in disco beat bars
They tried to lasso
secret buffaloes
We warned those wolves
who sought the weak
we were demented
and full of dog meat

They could not stop
our thoughts in the final blast
the radioactivity
of secrecy
and pulsation
of separate charts
A jump of the needle
on the Richter scale
played an album repeatedly
We danced behind a clay drum
throwing out flyers
Swirling broadsides
of yin and yang
confetti papers
we bought at the parade

The SOS
of the stranded
(our bodies)
called us
to our beds
small mats
in the corner
of a large cage

We knelt as primordial apes
and dared the other
to name creation
The language changed
at last
We entered
the final passage
and separated

SPEAKING HANDS

Our blind fingers
touch with the feet of birds
our palates and tongues.
Leaking deaf-toned words
I gape my mouth to swallow
cursed stones,
slight and bare.

The soft care of these hands
smooth them,
the numerous tales
of dragging necklaces
and distant walks.

I feel your fingernail
trace my ear, so as to hear again.
Wakened, I arise
from perch and wing
with burrs my flight
in this cloud, not my wordless throat
that lies and can be heard
so well through glass.

My blind hands speak
into our clasp, a tattoo on your palm.
Worn ridges that see
the internal sleep of my feet
talk of a new procession,

this rustle lain shallow
in the roots of my old woman's lips.

I have not yet spoken well,
senseless
with dark, clotted teeth
and the faint slide of this embrace.

I hear voices drink themselves
and clear hands clap bones
together in familiar rattle.
The raw tongues clop as hooves,
run in flood to recall my own gabble of tongues.
I have a damp palm over my breast
and it separates the nimble
little hearts that are freed
from my pores.

I cannot charm your fingers.
A stone is too much to ask you to take.
There is that path of mazes and mirrors.
I see this body caught in passage
through its own eggshell.

CUSTER MUST HAVE LEARNED TO DANCE

I am caught in the new power
of his dedicated motion.
Rolling in the cavalry money,
playing in the hands of Indian children.
I become an origami object
of horses, teepees and simple men.
They warp into vans, trendy clothes
and books on religious attitudes
to a dying planet.
I am taught within this nation
ideals of Greek platitudes,
an odyssey of epitomized frustrations.
Original sin, archetypes and eternity
are obsessions of dusty virtues.
Prattlers interlock with the loss
of ancestral homelands
birthing aboriginal psychosis.

SHE IS A STRANGER TO INTIMACY

She is mute and sign talks
between her ankles,
"deep inside Fannie Sprinkle."
Upstairs, she is warm rubber and malleable.
With steel-weighted tongue
she glistens, reptilian
on her 8 x 10 dance floor of sexual affront.
Passion flowers in her throat of cigarettes
and chest pain.

Synchronous flashes of red lights
on bridges wink
a twirling ball proclamation,
"TOP OF THE COSMOS,"
a herald sign of destination.
She reminds herself, the only way to cross
rivers are by those bridges,
to avoid the skydive ghosts of suicides
that linger in the fallen rainbows of oil stains.
Suitors parade as horses,
shift foot to foot, penises in salute
to the symmetry of another woman
who will bloat into female Sasquatch,
ugly and lonely at Waterfront.

She is glass disrupted by some break
of mental traffic, Grand
Avenue's cruising herd of metallic fireflies.

Oily smoke plumes to the exhausted clouds.
She is her toes crunched on spikes
and kicks the promise of crowns
that glitter from these street lamps.
She is one of the praying women
who eat their lovers slowly
from head down.
Without their silver, dollar bill heads
they are impatient to possess her.

She is power struck into black eyes,
into kowtows to ice cold looking glasses
of their tongue-licks and butt-wags.
Joints rock and grind Full Moon quarters
down her back through legs
that stagger female hips.
Too much of someone inside.
Flints spark on fragile piety and poise.
It is her holy body, then it is not.

She smells a 24-hour television.
She suspects it to be skin and sweat
singed in tangled wires.
She cackles and improvises a semblance
of personhood, steals the lips from the magazine
cover and recalls the origin of lipstick.
The French whores advertising willingness
to give head. Lips strong and taut
as babies on hard nipples.

She is exasperated.
Chasing down the street he opens his hand
to give her a French tickler.
She slaps it from his hand and winces,

"Thea! Thea, don't you leave me!"
He shouts, "I paid your drinks, woman!"
As proud Diva, she swaggers
past the solemn leer of money
into a flash of skirts.
With a thousand veils
she takes John's head to motels,
to moan over him like true love,
horrible victim songs,
Country Western.

He talks sometimes of her crazy doorways,
the stare of bikini panties stretched
over street signs and bared breasts.
Sights that scared him as she stuffed
him in her sequined purse.

She controls the nooses
that she fashions to reclaim
her innocence, her shame,
but cannot kill him.
He is her conquered,
a coup de grace to the groin.
Decapitated, he still insists on living
with her, but he is not a man.
He cannot reach for her.

In the morning, coffee cups
impress her face with many circles
like sleepmarks.
Her hair stands at ease.
She begins her regimen
of balms and bath.
She hears the street sweepers

flush the street.
She remembers the time they drenched her
with fire hoses between their legs.
They are like the other men.
They are so many hands
not one of them familiar.

A WARRIOR AND THE GLASS PRISONERS

I. The Glass Girl - a dream

I like what the soldiers give
if it shines or I see my face in it.
>Hiding in the grass.
>I haven't a name. My family is dead.
>Saddened, I have forgotten it is from this.
>Encircled, the soldier calls me.
>He named me Mona Glass, "Mona Glass,
>you and the women come back!
>We won't shoot. It will be better
>to come back than run."

He is a good man. He has many nice things.
He doesn't think of some faraway woman
when he touches me.
Maybe I am his wife.
He told me all the men
are put in cages,
somewhere, singing of death.
>The women say if we can get away we can find
>another land. Nothing can be done if we stay.
>Waiting for gifts and food from these Blue Men.
>Hearing the children cry and be sent off.
>Digging in the dirt.
>Dead is dead, without the spirit.
>I know this is against me. I do not dig in the dirt.
>I have spirit and my beauty and my presents.
>I think nothing can be done without the men.

I stand and wave my arms toward him.
The women run and the grass flattens from our fall.
I hold together the front of my dress
and all the mirrors I have sewn on
sparkle and break.

II. Don't Touch Me When I Sleep

I called her "Woman" in Cheyenne.
She was Vietnamese and young, very young.
She kept my hooch clean and cooked for me.
She rubbed my shoulders.
My name is John Hawk.
I drank and talked to her in my language.
> *She looked so familiar*
> *in the sweaty night.*
She made my hooch out of nothing, it seemed.
She made it look like a sweat lodge.
I sweated enough, but I am not clean yet.
I have killed so many people.
I killed a Grandmother because my C.O. said to.

"Kill her! Shoot or get shot in the back, Hawk!"
She could have a bomb in her bundle.
I shot her. I trembled so much, I hoped to miss.
She had little army tins in her sack,
cans she begged from good soldier boys,
like me. My woman didn't cry.
> *What is the battle, anyway? Am I in it now?*
> *It's dark. Her legs are smooth and feel good.*
I think about the Indian girls back home
who are afraid of me.
In their bones I know they remember.
One time I came back and she was gone.

Every girl I turned around looked like my younger sister.
I got drunk and shot up the little hooch.
I left it for good, all tore up.

> *I talk Vietnamese to the women.*
> *I am sure they remember 'Nam*
> *and that I killed their Grandmothers.*

I wear fatigues when I Traditional Dance
at the Veteran's Powwow.
My duffel bag is packed with everything I own.
I am waiting for someone to stop
and tell me to go home.

III. Don't Touch the Glass Girl

Mirrors are all around.
When I walk I see shadows
of myself, caught
in soft focus.
The capture is quick.
I am pure in glass,
untouched.

Not so, late at night when the trucks slow
to catch me walking home.
I am being called.
Grandmother says to come home.

There is a two-hundred-mile stretch of road,
over mountains, over snow.
Precipices have waterfalls
where heartsick women threw off
themselves
and landed pure-boned.

If I knew flesh had this pain
I would have stayed in the burning house
of my childhood.
I ran out plain and full of smoke.

Grandmother is tiny, unable to walk,
and doesn't hear how hard
it is to breathe.
I hold her hand,
so cold and large
from hard work.

You know how it is to be homeless.
Every time I awake
I hold still until I realize
where I am.
I am digging in the dirt.
For her, I am digging
for home.

The drivers say I have pretty hair.
I am hollow-cold from sleeping in the leaves.
Each one gives me a name to acknowledge,
numbers to call, when I can.
Left, I am glass
lying on the asphalt.

We used to have coffee together in the longhouse.
She told me about the Dreamer songs
and of the people back from death.
> *The light is pure.*
> *Our hearts are pure.*
> *We see God in this light.*
> *We are pure light in ourselves.*

Only the picture at my mother's house smiles.
Cheek taut, chin sharp,
my bones gleam through the descent.

I wander down the road at night.
Being called
I hear Celilo
singing under the dam waters.
I-84 is the coldest snake ever walked on.
Its eyes stop for me.
I crawl into each jaw
and shudder down the flat back
of the freeway.

COLD BLOOD

The arrow, he flies surely to this beating stone,
the woman displaced and stopped on the sidewalk.
In the City of Roses, flowers burst outward
as does her furious sorrow.
Small in the expanse, she has plunged
into the undertow,
wiping the streets with her back.
She has rolled out of moving vehicles,
off the biggest bridges, and survived,
but not this.
He is a silver lure spinning deceit.

There is red. There is blue.
Earth and sky.
Red is the sockeye flaming into the Snake River.
Cold-red flesh, blood cupped in the spine,
listens to the language of turmoil.
The final articulation of this blood will be spawning.
That is what she bites.

She moves her torso
slowly into this straight posture,
bending the clouds.
The mountain shawled like this has a gentle voice.
In her throat run the high desert antelope
and the air of quails.
The many feathers in her hands are eagles.
Before the grasses wave gold, the salmon, the *nusoox*,

search for the other in her hair.
Floating after the word, the word is love.
In the volcanic soil there is a short spring,
a brief season of flesh.

He is haunted and crumbles under ice and rain.
The common circle is strange.
His hands bear fragile weapons
to impale this moon, this earth.
He flays the petals from the stems, the nectar.
Juniper and pine whistle comfort her, the farewell song.

He leaves the body with stones in her palms,
obsidian in the belly,
in the current.
A thunderegg beats its heart from her mouth
into the river that she had left at birth.

HAND TO HAND, THE CIRCLES EMBRACE

Measured, your hands are as tall as fifteen horses.
Over me they are adequate shelter.
On my belly they gently find the serenity of a creek.

This is the return of your fish, your belly.
Wild palms are blind and read the course of blood.
Voiceless fingerlings, they draw together,
overwhelmed in these elements.

Your fist in my hold grow from the boy.
My portrait of you is the delighted shape of your eyes,
fingertips of shadows, the bow of a kiss.
I am the girl with submerged eyes that are creek rocks.

I recall our animal bed in the grass and cattails.
Smooth circles for the hands in a peacock parade.
The plod of fancy stature through dust.

Fingers are not enough through expanses of land or journey.
Hands are small compared to the miles of inches
added up from touch and the lost circles of time.

OUR REVERENCE AND DIFFICULT RETURN

"Hell, the first welfare handout happened at Plymouth Rock!
Every conservative should remember that."

"Every paycheck is a sellout, especially the ones
that are government green and land settlements."

These recollections are perishable,
summoned appearances of a lynched man
in Oklahoma and a Hopi-Tewa shot
in a Texas rest area.
In every territory there is a fully armed Posse Comitatus.
We are fugitives, silent with one another
in the sparse, corn-buildings.
Namoki, Hopi and Tewa, resembled 300 years
of Pueblo uprising and colored corn.
Shards rise from the kernels
that grow in the soil of his guardians
and Mimbres bowls.
Namoki ran revolt through adobe cells
of the New Mexico State Penitentiary.
Strewn about Oklahoma's robbed corpse,
trading beads twinkle as lost stars
and suffocate in black oil.
The stench, only we smell,
incenses the families
that lie in premature graves.

Multiple faces, paper-colored
and armored haunt us with flashing lights
and uniform blue. For them I wear this turquoise
to prevent broken bones.
The calcium heart I keep dropping
every time I drink beer.
I drink into an emotional hermit,
a priestess of bath pearls and suds.

You conceal opalescent kernels
of sorrow with enormous sleight of hand.
I have bowls of those myself.
I never dissolve them, except
in a hot, porcelain bath,
where I am alone.
Now, I am as red as the Bandelier cliffs.
The kiva is several hundred feet up
with only handholds carved in the ascent.
I still shake.

Every man and woman is singing tonight.
I know this from the full moon.
Cattails beat on car hoods.
Fluffs burst as insoluble down and dandelion
into our eyes. Our ducts tear and the moisture
slips through the road dust.
We are not crying this time.
Palms sanctimoniously rub the grains of pollen.
Hopefully, my lips are red enough
to remind you of those reservation bouffants
and women colored with dye as one-much-beloved
in the old days.

I rub off the obligatory lipstick
and reach outward again.
Heroes are rare, you are mine,
akimbo over me in a thousand form,
innumerable stars.

(No one saw them killed by police,
so it was not a crime, only suicide.)
We will rest on our canes,
full of medicine and herbs,
to watch our heroes return
over the deep sleep and sunrise.
Shaken from our lusts and coarse requirements
of survival, we will be roused from our helpless state.

It is only devotion
and the particular names
we give to faith that saves
us and those spirits
buried in the wrong manner,
not fetal and whole.
We pray for this world.
Is it corn pollen, this time,
that makes you cry?
Or is it the inability to reach them like this?

Condensed, we are a man and woman.
One of each, inside,
in this strata, upside down,
rolling over each other.
Like ivory, we are hard at the center
and soft as new antlers on the surface.
I can only comfort the hump of your back.

Warmed, I fill with simple pearls.
I will name all of my children
after landscapes
however they resemble and perpetuate
this ache.

NOTES ON THE POEMS

SPEELYAY THOUGHTS IN SEATTLE
Speelyay is Coyote, the trickster.

COYOTE FOLKLORE, IN IMAGE AND PRACTICE
Coyote Stories by Crystal Quintasket was originally published in 1933. An Okanogan writer, she was one of the first Native American women writers to publish fiction. A contemporary collection that includes Coyote stories is *Habu* by Vi Hilbert, an Upper Skagit storyteller and founder and director of Lushootseed Research and Press. Some Coyote story interpretations by non–Native American scholars are: *Shaking the Pumpkin* by Jerome Rothenberg; *Coyote Was Going There* by Jarold Ramsey; and *Giving Birth to Thunder, Sleeping with Daughter, Coyote Builds North America* by Barry Lopez.

SHE-WHO-WATCHES, THE NAMES ARE PRAYER
She-Who-Watches is a petroglyph on the Columbia River. She was originally a woman chief, the last, before Coyote changed her into rock to watch over her people and the male chiefs who followed her. Celilo Falls was the longest site of habitation for Indian people in the Northwest, an estimated fourteen thousand years. In 1957 it was sold to accommodate The Dalles Dam on the Columbia River.

ABOUT THE AUTHOR

ELIZABETH WOODY was born in Ganado, Arizona, in 1959. She is of Yakama, Warm Springs, Wasco, and Navajo descent and is an enrolled member of the Confederated Tribes of Warm Springs, Oregon. She studied creative writing at the Institute of American Indian Arts in Santa Fe and Portland State University and later earned her B.A. from Evergreen State College. She is a cofounder of the Northwest Native American Writers Association. She currently teaches writing at the Institute of American Indian Arts. A visual artist as well as a writer, her work has been shown in several national and international touring exhibitions and in galleries throughout the Northwest. Recently, her work was included in the limited edition 1994 *Reflex* Portfolio of prints by contemporary Native American artists produced by the master printmaker, Elizabeth Tapper, in Seattle, Washington. In 1990, her first book, *Hand into Stone,* received the American Book Award from the Before Columbus Foundation. Her second book, *Luminaries of the Humble,* a collection of poetry, was published by the University of Arizona Press in 1994. *Seven Hands, Seven Hearts* is her third book. She makes her home in both Santa Fe, New Mexico and Portland, Oregon.

ABOUT THE ARTIST WHOSE WORK IS ON THE COVER

RICK BARTOW is an artist of Yurok descent. One of the central themes of his art is the concept of transformations. He has spoken of them in his own psychological recovery, in the crossings between animals and people, and in the mixture of everyday emotions of the moment. Several figures and characters turn up repeatedly: Coyote, Crow, and Hawk especially. Bartow describes the close connections between animals and humans: "In Yurok mythology, not unlike many other people's mythology, there are always animals who are given voices like people. So in a sense, you see animals as being people and people as being animals." His work has been shown in numerous solo and group exhibitions in the U.S. and internationally. He was born on the coast of Oregon at Newport, not far from his ancestral lands in northern California. He lives today, with his family, in the same house in which he grew up. Rick Bartow and Elizabeth Woody met in 1985. He describes her work as "charged" and thinks of Elizabeth as a woman whose concerns are for others and whose laughter is infectious. The cover art, "Wajima Hawk," is pastel and graphite on paper, 42" x 50", 1992. Rick Bartow is represented by the Jamison/Thomas Gallery in Portland, Oregon.

ABOUT THE ARTIST WHOSE DRAWINGS ARE IN THE BOOK

JAUNE QUICK-TO-SEE SMITH is a member of the Flathead tribe, Montana. She is an activist/spokesperson for contemporary Native American artists. Most recently, her paintings appeared in "Myth and Magic in the Americas," at the Museo de Arte Contemporanea de Monterrey, Mexico, a major survey of painters in the Western Hemisphere. She was also one of six featured artists for the 52nd Presidential Commemorative Inaugural poster. She has completed public art projects at the Yerba Buena Gardens (Moscone Center), San Francisco, and the main terminal terrazzo floor of the new Denver airport. Her activities also include assisting in the design of a Cultural Museum on the Flathead Reservation and serving as a member of the design team for the National Museum of the American Indian. She lectures and is a visiting artist at colleges and universities nationwide. Smith's work appears in numerous publications, including the books *Mixed Blessings* and *Partial Recall* by Lucy Lippard. Her work has been the subject of three PBS films, as well as German and Finnish documentaries. She currently resides in Corrales, New Mexico.